JUST **4** INGREDIENTS

JUST 4 INGREDIENTS

Love Food ® is an imprint of
Parragon Books Ltd

Parragon
Queen Street House
4 Queen Street
Bath BA1 1HE, UK

Love Food ® and the accompanying heart
device is a trademark of Parragon Books Ltd

Design: Terry Jeavons & Company
Photography: Mike Cooper
Home economist: Lincoln Jefferson

ISBN 978-1-4075-4911-8

Printed in China

This book uses metric and imperial
measurements. Follow the same units of
measurement throughout; do not mix metric
and imperial. All spoon measurements are
level, unless otherwise stated: teaspoons
are assumed to be 5ml, and tablespoons
are assumed to be 15ml. Unless otherwise
stated, milk is assumed to be full fat, eggs
and individual fruits such as bananas are
medium, and pepper is freshly ground
black pepper.

Recipes using raw or very lightly cooked eggs
should be avoided by children, the elderly,
pregnant women, convalescents, and anyone
suffering from an illness. Pregnant and
breast-feeding women are advised to avoid
eating peanuts and peanut products.

Contents

Introduction 6

1   Soups, Starters & Snacks 8

2   Fish & Seafood 38

3   Meat & Poultry 76

4   Vegetables & Vegetarian Dishes 112

5   Desserts 146

Index 176

Introduction

For everyday eating, nothing beats home cooking for flavour, variety, nutrition and cost. However, real life isn't like being a celebrity chef on television, as you are the one who has to do all the shopping, preparation, cooking and even clearing up afterwards, while trying to balance work and family life and, maybe, even squeezing in a few minutes of time for yourself. Buying the weekly groceries doesn't have to take the major part of your precious hours off and preparing and cooking delicious, healthy meals doesn't have to be a time-consuming chore.

Using just four ingredients – excluding water, salt and pepper, any accompaniments such as dipping sauces and crisp breads, and optional garnishes – cuts down the amount of time you have to spend shopping and preparing food yet will still result in tasty and nutritious meals. As well as saving time – one of our rarest commodities nowadays – these recipes make choice easier. Many people find a long list of ingredients, followed by a mass of instructions, bewildering and it may be difficult to tell whether you'll actually like the dish once you've cooked it. If there are only four ingredients, you'll have a pretty clear idea of what the characteristic flavour will be and even the inexperienced cook will be confident of success.

Perhaps the most surprising thing about the recipes in this book is the sheer variety of dishes you can create with just four ingredients. They range from great midweek family suppers to quick after-school snacks and light lunches and from hearty stews, roasts and bakes to impressively elegant dinner-party dishes. There is a chapter devoted to each course: Soups, Starters & Snacks, Fish & Seafood, Meat & Poultry, Vegetables & Vegetarian Dishes and Desserts. Within each chapter, you'll find recipes to suit all tastes, occasions and household budgets.

Using the best-quality ingredients is one of the keys to success with any kind of cooking, but it is perhaps especially important when there are only four of them. This doesn't necessarily mean that they have to cost more. Indeed, many of the recipes in this book are very economical. There are still debates on whether organic ingredients taste better than conventional produce and you will have to make up your own mind about that. What is well established is that freshness is the star factor for flavour. Wherever possible, buy local and seasonal ingredients, which will taste better and will often retain more of their nutrients. Remember that flavour and aroma count for more than appearance.

1

Soups, Starters & Snacks

Home-made soups are always welcome, whether in a steaming bowl in winter or chilled for an alfresco lunch in summer, and the great thing is that they are very easy to make. This chapter also includes tempting snacks and starters that are great for both family meals and for entertaining.

Beef Consommé with Eggs and Parmesan

INGREDIENTS

main

1.5 litres/2¾ pints beef consommé or beef stock

3 eggs

25 g/1 oz fresh white breadcrumbs

55 g/2 oz Parmesan cheese, freshly grated

storecupboard

salt

serves ❹

1 Pour the consommé or stock into a saucepan and heat gently, stirring occasionally.

2 Meanwhile, beat the eggs in a bowl until combined, then stir in the breadcrumbs and Parmesan. Season with salt.

3 As soon as the consommé or stock comes to the boil, add the egg mixture. When it floats to the surface, stir with a fork to break it up. Ladle into warmed soup bowls and then serve immediately.

Spinach & Cheese Soup

INGREDIENTS

main

225 g/8 oz fresh baby spinach leaves, tough stalks removed

600 ml/1 pint milk

700 ml/1¼ pints vegetable or chicken stock

200 g/7 oz Boursin or other cream cheese flavoured with garlic and herbs

storecupboard

salt and pepper

croûtons (optional)

serves 6 to 8

1 Put the spinach in a large saucepan and pour in the milk and stock. Bring to the boil, then reduce the heat and simmer gently for 12 minutes. Remove the pan from the heat and leave to cool completely.

2 Ladle the cold soup into a food processor, in batches if necessary, and process until smooth. Cut the cheese into chunks and add to the soup. Process again until smooth and creamy.

3 Pour the soup into a bowl and season to taste with salt and pepper. Cover with clingfilm and leave to chill in the refrigerator for at least 3 hours. Stir well before ladling into bowls. Add croûtons, if using, and serve immediately.

Easy Asparagus Soup

INGREDIENTS

main

425 g/15 oz canned asparagus spears

25 g/1 oz butter

2 tbsp plain flour

600 ml/1 pint milk

storecupboard

salt and pepper

serves 4

1 Drain the asparagus, reserving the can juices. Cut the asparagus spears into short lengths and set aside.

2 Melt the butter in a saucepan over a low heat. Stir in the flour and cook, stirring constantly, for 1 minute. Remove the pan from the heat.

3 Gradually stir in the reserved can juices, then slowly stir in the milk. Return the pan to the heat and bring to the boil, stirring constantly. Add the asparagus spears and heat through gently for 2–3 minutes.

4 Ladle the soup into a food processor, in batches if necessary, and process until smooth. Stir well before ladling into bowls. Season with pepper, and salt if necessary, and serve.

Cream of Pea Soup

INGREDIENTS

main

115 g/4 oz butter

1 onion, finely chopped

450 g/1 lb shelled peas

600–700 ml/1–1¼ pints milk

storecupboard

150 ml/5 fl oz water

salt and pepper

serves ❹

1 Melt the butter in a saucepan over a low heat. Add the onion and cook, stirring occasionally, for 5 minutes until softened.

2 Add the peas and pour in the water. Increase the heat to medium and simmer for 3–4 minutes, or until the peas are tender. (Frozen peas will be ready in 10 minutes.)

3 Add 600 ml/1 pint of the milk, season with salt and pepper and then bring to the boil, stirring constantly.

4 Remove the pan from the heat and leave to cool slightly, then pour the soup into a food processor and process to a smooth purée.

5 Return the soup to the rinsed-out pan and bring back to the boil. If the soup seems too thick, heat the remaining milk in a small saucepan and stir it into the soup. Taste and adjust the seasoning if necessary, and serve.

Leek & Potato Soup

INGREDIENTS

serves 4

main

55 g/2 oz butter

4 leeks, trimmed and chopped

350 g/12 oz potatoes, diced

850 ml/1½ pints chicken or vegetable stock

storecupboard

salt and pepper

extra virgin olive oil, for drizzling (optional)

1 Melt half the butter in a saucepan over a low heat. Add the leeks and cook, stirring occasionally, for 5 minutes until softened.

2 Add the potatoes and cook, stirring occasionally, for 3 minutes. Increase the heat to medium, pour in the stock and bring to the boil. Reduce the heat, cover and simmer for 35–40 minutes, or until the leeks and potatoes are tender.

3 Remove the pan from the heat and stir in the remaining butter in small pieces at a time. Season to taste with salt and pepper. Press the soup through a sieve or pass through a food mill into a warmed bowl. Alternatively, ladle the soup straight into a bowl to leave it with a chunky texture. Serve immediately, drizzled with extra virgin olive oil, if using.

Avocado Soup

INGREDIENTS

main

1 litre/1¾ pints chicken or vegetable stock

225 ml/8 fl oz double cream

2 large avocados

2 tbsp finely chopped fresh chives

storecupboard

salt and pepper

Tabasco sauce (optional)

serves 4

1 Pour the stock and cream into a saucepan and bring to just below boiling point over a low heat.

2 Halve the avocados and remove the stones. Using a fork, mash the flesh in the half shells, then scoop out into a bowl. Pour the stock mixture into the mashed avocado, whisking constantly with a balloon whisk.

3 Season to taste with salt and pepper and leave to cool, then cover with clingfilm and chill in the refrigerator for 2–3 hours. Stir the soup and serve sprinkled with the chives and dotted with Tabasco sauce, if using.

Red Pepper & Orange Soup

INGREDIENTS

main

5 blood oranges

3 tbsp olive oil

1.5 kg/3 lb 5 oz red peppers, deseeded and sliced

1½ tbsp orange flower water

storecupboard

salt and pepper

extra virgin olive oil, for drizzling (optional)

serves ❹

1 Finely grate the rind of one of the oranges and shred the rind of another with a citrus zester. Set aside. Squeeze the juice from all the oranges.

2 Heat the oil in a saucepan, add the red peppers and cook over a medium heat, stirring occasionally, for 10 minutes. Stir in the grated orange rind and cook for a further few minutes. Reduce the heat, cover and simmer gently, stirring occasionally, for 20 minutes.

3 Remove the pan from the heat, leave to cool slightly, then transfer the red pepper mixture to a food processor and process to a smooth purée. Add the orange juice and orange flower water and process again until thoroughly combined.

4 Transfer the soup to a bowl, season to taste with salt and leave to cool completely, then cover with clingfilm and chill in the refrigerator for 3 hours. Stir well before serving sprinkled with the shredded orange rind and drizzled with extra virgin olive oil, if using.

Bacon Rolls

INGREDIENTS

main

9 baby leeks

9 thin slices of lean back bacon

1 tbsp cornflour

1½ tbsp sunflower oil

storecupboard

salt and pepper

serves ❹

1 Trim the baby leeks to the same length, then blanch in a saucepan of salted boiling water for 2 minutes. Drain and refresh in cold water, then drain again.

2 Put 3 slices of bacon side by side on a clean work surface, overlapping them slightly. Brush lightly with a little cornflour. Place 3 leeks, alternating the bulb and leaf ends, at one end of the bacon and roll up securely. Tie with kitchen string. Repeat with the remaining bacon, cornflour and leeks.

3 Heat the oil in a frying pan, add the bacon rolls and cook over a medium-low heat, turning frequently, for 6–8 minutes until the bacon is cooked through and lightly coloured.

4 Remove the rolls with a slotted spoon and drain on kitchen paper. Remove and discard the string and cut the rolls into slices about 1 cm/½ inch thick. Arrange in a warmed dish, season with pepper and serve immediately.

Ham & Asparagus Rolls

INGREDIENTS

serves **6**

main

6 large slices cooked ham

425 g/15 oz canned asparagus spears, drained

300 ml/10 fl oz condensed asparagus or mushroom soup

140 g/5 oz Gruyère cheese, grated

1 Preheat the oven to 180°C/350°F/Gas Mark 4. Spread out the slices of ham and divide the asparagus spears among them. Roll up the ham to wrap around the spears and put the rolls in an ovenproof dish.

2 Pour the condensed soup into a saucepan and heat gently, without adding any extra liquid, but do not allow it to boil. When the soup is hot, remove the pan from the heat and stir in the grated cheese until melted.

3 Pour the soup over the ham rolls and bake for 20 minutes, or until hot and bubbling. Serve immediately straight from the dish.

Chorizo with Parsley & Olives

INGREDIENTS

main

650 g/1 lb 7 oz chorizo sausage, cut into 5-mm/¼-inch slices

1 tbsp olive oil

bunch of fresh flat-leaf parsley, chopped

85 g/3 oz black olives

serves **6**

1 Heat a large, heavy-based frying pan, add the chorizo slices and cook over a medium heat, turning and stirring frequently, for 5 minutes until crisp. Remove from the pan with a fish slice or spatula and drain well on kitchen paper. Discard the fat remaining in the pan.

2 Heat the oil in the frying pan, add the cooked chorizo slices, parsley and olives and cook, stirring constantly, for 3–4 minutes, or until heated through. Serve immediately.

Tomato Bruschetta

INGREDIENTS

serves **4**

main

8 slices of rustic bread

4 garlic cloves, halved

8 plum tomatoes, peeled and diced

extra virgin olive oil, for drizzling

storecupboard

salt and pepper

fresh basil leaves, to garnish (optional)

1 Preheat the grill. Lightly toast the bread on both sides. Rub each piece of toast with half a garlic clove and then return to the grill for a few seconds.

2 Divide the diced tomatoes among the toasts. Season to taste with salt and pepper and drizzle with olive oil. Serve immediately, garnished with basil leaves, if using.

Nachos with Chillies & Olives

INGREDIENTS

main

1 kg/2 lb 4 oz tortilla chips

6 tbsp chopped pickled jalapeño chillies

115 g/4 oz black olives, stoned and sliced

450 g/1 lb Cheddar cheese, grated

storecupboard

dipping sauce

serves ❹

1 Preheat the oven to 180°C/350°F/Gas Mark 4. Spread out the tortilla chips in a large ovenproof dish.

2 Sprinkle the chillies, olives and grated cheese evenly over the tortilla chips and bake for 12–15 minutes, or until the cheese is melted and bubbling. Serve immediately with a dipping sauce of your choice.

Aubergine Pâté

INGREDIENTS

main

2 large aubergines

4 tbsp extra virgin olive oil

2 garlic cloves, very finely chopped

4 tbsp lemon juice

storecupboard

salt and pepper

6 crisp breads

serves ❹ to ❻

1 Preheat the oven to 180°C/350°F/Gas Mark 4. Score the skins of the aubergines with the point of a sharp knife, without piercing the flesh, and place them on a baking sheet. Bake for 1¼ hours, or until soft.

2 Remove the aubergines from the oven and leave until cool enough to handle. Cut them in half and, using a spoon, scoop out the flesh into a bowl. Mash the flesh thoroughly.

3 Gradually beat in the olive oil then stir in the garlic and lemon juice. Season to taste with salt and pepper. Cover with clingfilm and store in the refrigerator until required. Serve with the crisp breads.

Artichokes with Parsley Butter

INGREDIENTS

main

4 globe artichokes

115 g/4 oz butter

2 garlic cloves, finely chopped

2 tbsp fresh flat-leaf parsley, chopped

storecupboard

salt

serves ❹

1 Break off the stems of the artichokes and cut off the top 1 cm/½ inch of the head with a sharp knife. Using kitchen scissors, cut off the points of the remaining leaves.

2 Put the artichokes in a saucepan and add water to cover and a pinch of salt. Bring to the boil, then reduce the heat, cover and simmer for 45 minutes, or until cooked. Test by gently pulling a lower leaf. If it comes away easily, the artichoke is ready. Drain well and place upside down on kitchen paper.

3 Melt the butter in a small saucepan over a low heat. Add the garlic and cook, stirring constantly, for 30 seconds. Remove the pan from the heat and stir in the parsley. Pour the herb butter into a small serving bowl. Place the artichokes, right way up, on serving plates and serve with the butter.

2 Fish & Seafood

Fish is invariably at its best when cooked simply with complementary rather than overpowering flavours, so it's the perfect choice for discovering the versatility of using just four ingredients. From Japanese-style tuna to family bakes, and from spicy prawns to creamy mussels, you will be spoilt for choice.

Plaice in Cream Sauce

INGREDIENTS

main

800 g/1 lb 12 oz plaice fillets

55 g/2 oz butter, melted

225 ml/8 fl oz crème fraîche

55 g/2 oz Cheddar cheese, grated

storecupboard

salt and pepper

fresh parsley, chopped, to garnish (optional)

serves ❹

1 Preheat the grill. If the plaice fillets have not already been skinned, you can do this yourself if you prefer. Anchor a fillet to a chopping board with a little salt. Insert the blade of a sharp knife at the tail end and then, holding the skin securely and with the knife blade at an angle, gradually cut the fillet away from the skin with a sawing motion. Repeat with the remaining fillets.

2 Brush the tops of the fillets with melted butter and cook under the grill for 6 minutes. Remove the grill pan and spread each fillet with crème fraîche and sprinkle evenly with the grated cheese.

3 Return the fish to the grill and cook for 1–2 minutes, or until the cheese has melted. Serve immediately, seasoned with pepper and garnished with chopped parsley, if using.

Baked Snapper

INGREDIENTS

serves **4**

main

2 bunches fresh basil

85 g/3 oz unsalted butter, softened

4 garlic cloves, crushed

4 red snapper or red mullet, about 350 g/12 oz each, scaled, trimmed and cleaned

storecupboard

salt and pepper

1 Preheat the oven to 180°C/350°F/Gas Mark 4. Cut out 4 double thickness squares of foil each large enough to hold a whole fish.

2 Reserve 4 basil sprigs for the garnish and chop the remaining leaves. Cream the butter in a bowl with a wooden spoon, then beat in the chopped basil and the garlic.

3 Season the fish inside and out with salt and pepper. Put a fish on a double thickness square of foil. Spoon one-quarter of the basil and garlic butter into the cavity and wrap the foil around the fish to enclose it completely. Repeat with the remaining fish.

4 Put the fish parcels on a large baking sheet and bake for 25–30 minutes, or until the fish flakes easily when tested with the point of a knife. Transfer the fish parcels to warmed plates and unwrap. Carefully slide out the fish and the cooking juices onto the plates, and serve immediately.

Oven-baked Swordfish Steaks

INGREDIENTS

main

4 swordfish steaks, about 200 g/7 oz each

2 lemons or 3 limes

55 g/2 oz butter

8 canned artichoke hearts

storecupboard

salt and pepper

serves ❹

1 Preheat the oven to 180°C/350°F/Gas Mark 4. Cut out 4 double thickness squares of foil, each large enough to hold the fish steaks.

2 Put a fish steak on each of the squares and fold up the sides until partly enclosed. Season with salt and pepper. Squeeze the juice from 1 of the lemons or 1½ of the limes. Cut the butter into quarters and place a quarter on each piece of fish. Top each steak with 2 artichoke hearts and divide the juice among the parcels.

3 Fold over the foil to seal in the juice, and put the parcels on a large baking sheet. Bake for 25 minutes, or until the flesh flakes easily when tested with the point of a knife.

4 Meanwhile, slice the remaining lemon or limes. Transfer the fish parcels to warmed serving plates, open the tops and garnish with the lemon or lime slices. Serve immediately.

Griddled Salmon with Cheese

INGREDIENTS

serves 4

main

4 salmon fillets, about 200 g/7 oz each

4 slices of Taleggio cheese, rind removed

8 fresh sage leaves

8 slices of prosciutto

storecupboard

salt and pepper

extra virgin olive oil, for drizzling (optional)

1 Season the fish with salt and pepper. Cut the cheese slices to fit the top of the salmon fillets and place them on the fish. Put 2 sage leaves on top of each cheese-topped fillet, then wrap each fillet in 2 slices of prosciutto.

2 Heat a ridged griddle pan. Add the wrapped fish fillets and cook over a medium heat for 5 minutes. Using a fish slice or spatula, carefully turn over each fillet and cook for a further 5 minutes.

3 Transfer the wrapped salmon fillets to warmed serving plates. Serve immediately, drizzled with extra virgin olive oil, if using.

Salmon & Herbs in Prosciutto Parcels

INGREDIENTS

serves **4**

main

**2 bunches of mixed fresh
herbs, such as coriander,
parsley, basil and dill**

**125–175 ml/4–6 fl oz extra
virgin olive oil**

**4 salmon fillets, about
200 g/7 oz each**

8 slices of prosciutto

storecupboard

salt and pepper

1 Preheat the oven to 180°C/350°F/Gas Mark 4.
Roughly chop the mixed herbs and put in a
mortar, season with a little salt and pound with
a pestle. Gradually work in the olive oil to make
a thick paste.

2 Spread the herb paste evenly over the tops
of the salmon fillets, then wrap each fillet in
2 slices of prosciutto.

3 Put the wrapped fillets on a large baking
sheet and bake for 20–25 minutes. Transfer to
warmed serving plates and serve immediately.

Sole with Mushrooms

INGREDIENTS

serves **4**

main

85 g/3 oz unsalted butter, plus extra for greasing

8 sole fillets, about 85 g/3 oz each

juice of 1 lemon

115 g/4 oz chanterelle mushrooms, torn into thin strips

storecupboard

salt and pepper

1 Preheat the oven to 190°C/375°F/Gas Mark 5. Grease an ovenproof dish with butter.

2 Season the fish fillets with salt and pepper, spread the tops with half the butter and sprinkle with the lemon juice. Put 4 fillets in the prepared dish and top with an even layer of mushrooms. Place the remaining fillets on top and dot with the remaining butter.

3 Cover the dish with a lid or sheet of foil, put on a baking sheet and bake for 20 minutes, or until the flesh flakes easily when tested with the point of a knife. Serve immediately, straight from the dish.

Marinated Monkfish Kebabs

INGREDIENTS

main

50 ml/2 fl oz olive oil

2 tbsp lemon juice

1½ tsp chopped fresh marjoram or oregano

550 g/1 lb 4 oz monkfish fillet, cut into 2.5-cm/1-inch cubes

storecupboard

salt and pepper

serves ❹

1 Mix the oil, lemon juice and marjoram together in a non-metallic dish and season with salt and pepper. Add the monkfish cubes and turn to coat. Leave to marinate for 30 minutes.

2 Preheat the grill. Drain the monkfish and thread the cubes onto 8 pre-soaked wooden skewers. Place under the grill and cook, turning frequently, for 3–5 minutes, or until the flesh flakes easily when tested with the point of a knife. Serve immediately.

Swordfish with a Crisp Tomato Topping

INGREDIENTS

main

4 swordfish or tuna steaks, about 175 g/6 oz each

3 tomatoes, sliced

70 g/2½ oz fresh multigrain breadcrumbs

grated rind and juice of 1½ lemons

storecupboard

pepper

lemon wedges (optional)

serves ❹

1 Preheat the oven to 200°C/400°F/Gas Mark 6. Arrange the fish steaks in an ovenproof dish in a single layer and cover with the tomato slices.

2 Mix the breadcrumbs and with the lemon rind and juice in a bowl and spoon the mixture evenly over the tomatoes.

3 Place the dish on a baking sheet and bake for 20–25 minutes, or until the fish flakes easily when tested with the point of a knife. Serve immediately straight from the dish, seasoned with pepper and garnished with lemon wedges, if using.

Skate with Caper Berries

INGREDIENTS

main

4 skate wings, about 225 g/8 oz each, skinned and trimmed

1½ tbsp olive oil

3 tbsp caper berries or capers, rinsed

grated rind and juice of 1 orange

storecupboard

pepper

lemon wedges (optional)

serves 4

1 Heat a ridged griddle pan. Pat the skate wings dry with kitchen paper. Brush both sides of the skate wings with the oil, add to the pan and cook over a high heat for 3–4 minutes on each side, depending on the thickness of the wings.

2 Reduce the heat and sprinkle the fish with the caper berries, orange rind and juice. Cook for a further 1 minute and season to taste with salt and pepper. Serve immediately straight from the dish, seasoned with pepper and garnished with lemon wedges, if using.

Teriyaki Tuna

INGREDIENTS

main

**4 tuna steaks, about
175 g/6 oz each**

6 tbsp sake

6 tbsp mirin

**6 tbsp shoyu (Japanese
soy sauce)**

serves ❹

1 Arrange the tuna steaks in a single layer in
a shallow dish. Mix the sake, mirin and shoyu
together in a jug. Pour the mixture over the
fish, turning to coat, then cover with clingfilm
and leave to marinate in the refrigerator for
6–8 hours.

2 Preheat the grill. Drain the tuna, reserving
the marinade. Put the fish on a grill rack and
cook, brushing frequently with the reserved
marinade, for 2–4 minutes on each side,
depending on how well done you like your tuna.
Alternatively, you can cook the fish on a
barbecue.

3 Pour any remaining marinade into a small
saucepan and bring just to the boil, then
remove the pan from the heat. Serve the tuna
hot with the warmed sauce.

Baked Fish with Preserved Lemons

INGREDIENTS

serves **4**

main

1 sea bream or sea bass, about 1.5 kg/3 lb 5 oz, trimmed, scaled and cleaned

2 tbsp chopped fresh coriander

1 tbsp sweet paprika

large jar of lemons preserved in oil

storecupboard

salt and pepper

1 Preheat the oven to 240°C/475°F/Gas Mark 9. Using a sharp knife, slash the fish diagonally 3–4 times on each side. Season the fish inside and out with salt and pepper. Put the coriander in the cavity and rub the paprika all over the outside of the fish.

2 Drain about 20 lemon slices and put 10–12 in the base of an ovenproof dish large enough to hold the fish. Place the fish on top and cover with the remaining drained lemon slices. Measure 150 ml/5 fl oz of the oil from the jar of lemons and pour it over the fish.

3 Put the dish on a large baking sheet and bake for 5 minutes, then reduce the oven temperature to 180°C/350°F/Gas Mark 4 and bake, basting frequently, for a further 40–45 minutes, or until the flesh flakes easily when tested with the point of a knife. Serve immediately straight from the dish.

Sea Bream with Tomatoes, Yogurt & Spinach

INGREDIENTS

serves 6

main

650 g/1 lb 7 oz fresh spinach leaves, tough stalks removed

6 sea bream fillets, about 175 g/6 oz each

6 tbsp Greek-style yogurt

6 tomatoes, peeled, deseeded and diced

storecupboard

salt and pepper

extra virgin olive oil, for drizzling (optional)

1 Preheat the oven to 230°C/450°F/Gas Mark 8. Blanch the spinach in a saucepan of salted boiling water for 1 minute. Drain well, squeezing out as much liquid as possible, and pat dry with kitchen paper. Reserve.

2 Season the fish fillets with salt and pepper. Arrange overlapping spinach leaves into 6 sheets large enough to enclose a fillet. Place a fillet on each spinach sheet and spoon 1 tablespoon of yogurt on top of each one. Divide the diced tomatoes among the fish fillets and wrap the spinach leaves over to enclose them completely.

3 Carefully transfer the spinach-wrapped fish to an ovenproof dish, arranging them in a single layer. Put on a baking sheet and bake for 10–15 minutes, or until the flesh flakes easily when tested with the point of a knife. Serve immediately, drizzled with extra virgin olive oil, if using.

Normandy Cream Mussels

INGREDIENTS

serves **4**

main

2 kg/4 lb 8 oz live mussels

300 ml/10 fl oz dry cider

6 shallots, finely chopped

6 tbsp double cream

storecupboard

pepper

1 Scrub the mussels under cold running water, scraping off any barnacles with a knife, and pull off the beards. Discard any mussels with broken shells or open ones that do not shut immediately when tapped sharply with the handle of a knife.

2 Pour the cider into a flameproof casserole dish, add the shallots and season with pepper. Bring to the boil and cook for 2 minutes.

3 Add the mussels, cover with a tight-fitting lid and cook over a high heat, shaking the casserole dish occasionally, for about 5 minutes until the shells have opened. Remove the mussels with a slotted spoon, discarding any that remain closed, and keep warm.

4 Strain the cooking liquid through a muslin-lined sieve into a saucepan. Bring to the boil and cook for 8–10 minutes until reduced by about half. Stir in the cream and add the mussels. Cook for 1 minute to reheat the shellfish, then serve in warmed bowls.

Mussels with Garlic & Parsley Butter

INGREDIENTS

main

3 large garlic cloves

175 g/6 oz unsalted butter, softened

55 g/2 oz fresh parsley, chopped

2 kg/4 lb 8 oz live mussels

storecupboard

salt and pepper

serves ❹

1 Place the garlic cloves on a board and flatten with the blade of a knife. Add a large pinch of salt and crush to a paste. Beat the paste into the butter in a bowl, add the parsley and season with pepper. Shape into a cylinder, wrap in greaseproof paper and chill in the refrigerator.

2 Scrub the mussels under cold running water, and pull off the beards. Discard any broken shells or open ones that do not shut immediately when tapped sharply with the handle of a knife.

3 Preheat the grill. Push the tip of a small sharp knife between each mussel shell on the straight side. Run the knife around between the shells, then ease back the top shell. Run the knife around the inside edge of the top shell, pull it back and snap it off.

4 Arrange the half shells in a single layer in a flameproof dish. Dot the mussel flesh with the butter. Cook under the grill for 5–8 minutes, or until the mussels are lightly browned and the butter has melted. Serve immediately.

Scallops in Vermouth

INGREDIENTS

main

1 kg/2 lb 4 oz shelled fresh scallops

55 g/2 oz unsalted butter

4 tbsp Noilly Prat or other dry vermouth

3 tbsp chopped fresh flat-leaf parsley

storecupboard

salt and pepper

serves ❹

1 If necessary, rinse the scallops and pat dry with kitchen paper. Season them with salt and pepper.

2 Melt 15 g/½ oz of the butter in a large frying pan. When it's just beginning to colour, add half the scallops and cook, turning occasionally, for 4–5 minutes until light golden brown on both sides. Remove from the pan and keep warm. Melt another 15 g/½ oz of the butter in the frying pan and cook the remaining scallops in the same way, then remove them from the pan and keep warm.

3 Add the Noilly Prat to the pan and stir in the remaining butter. When it has melted, stir in the parsley and pour the sauce over the scallops. Serve immediately, seasoned with pepper.

Mustard Prawns

INGREDIENTS

main

20–24 raw tiger prawns

55 g/2 oz unsalted butter

225 ml/8 fl oz double cream

1 tbsp Dijon mustard

storecupboard

salt and pepper

serves ❹

1 Pull off the heads from the prawns and peel them. Make an incision along the back of each prawn with a small sharp knife and carefully remove the dark vein with the point of the knife.

2 Melt the butter in a large frying pan, add the prawns and cook, stirring frequently, for 3–4 minutes. Pour in the cream, season with salt and pepper and stir in the mustard. Simmer gently over a low heat for a further 5 minutes. Serve immediately.

Prawns in Orange Juice

INGREDIENTS

serves **6**

main

3 red peppers

30–36 large raw prawns

2 tbsp olive oil

juice of 1 large orange

storecupboard

salt and pepper

1 Preheat the grill. Put the peppers on a baking sheet and cook under the grill, turning frequently, until the skins are blistered and charred. Using tongs, transfer to a polythene bag, tie the top and leave until cool enough to handle.

2 Meanwhile, pull off the heads from the prawns and peel them. Make an incision along the back of each prawn with a small sharp knife and carefully remove the dark vein with the point of the knife.

3 When the peppers are cool enough to handle, peel off the skins, then halve and deseed them. Cut the flesh into thin strips.

4 Heat the oil in a large frying pan, add the pepper strips, season with salt and pepper, cover and cook over a low heat, for 5 minutes. Add the prawns and cook, stirring occasionally, for 3–4 minutes, then pour in the orange juice and simmer for a further 2–3 minutes until the prawns are tender. Taste and adjust the seasoning, if necessary, and serve.

Hot Chilli Prawns

INGREDIENTS

main

3–4 fresh green chillies

juice of 1 lime

2 tbsp groundnut oil

24 raw tiger prawns

storecupboard

pepper

serves 4

1 Deseed the chillies if you prefer a milder flavour, then chop roughly. Put the chillies, lime juice and oil in a food processor and process until thoroughly combined. Pour the mixture into a non-metallic dish.

2 Pull off the heads from the prawns and peel them. Make an incision along the back of each prawn with a small sharp knife and carefully remove the dark vein with the point of the knife. Add the prawns to the dish and stir to coat. Cover with clingfilm and leave to marinate for 30 minutes.

3 Preheat the grill. Drain the prawns, reserving the marinade, and thread them onto 6 skewers. Cook under the grill, turning frequently and brushing with the marinade, for 5 minutes, until tender. Alternatively, you can cook the prawns on a barbecue. Serve immediately, seasoned with pepper.

3 Meat & Poultry

Whether special-occasion dishes with the choicest cuts, or inexpensive family suppers based on more economical meats, these fabulous dishes are sure to please. It's hard to believe that tasty stews, braises and roasts, spicy chicken, and fruity duck breasts simply result from the ingenious combination of just four ingredients.

Peppered Steak

INGREDIENTS

main

4 tbsp green peppercorns

**4 sirloin steaks, about
225 g/8 oz each, trimmed**

115 g/4 oz butter

2 tbsp brandy

serves **4**

1 Press the peppercorns into both sides of the steaks. Place on a plate, cover and leave to stand for 1 hour.

2 Heat a large, heavy-based frying pan, add the butter and, as soon as it has melted, add the steaks. Cook for 2–4 minutes on each side, until cooked to your liking. Remove the steaks with a spatula and keep warm.

3 Add the brandy to the pan and stir well to mix. Spoon the sauce over the steaks and serve immediately.

Stuffed Beef Fillet

INGREDIENTS

serves ❹

main

**1 beef fillet, about
600 g/1 lb 5 oz**

**5 tbsp finely chopped
sun-dried tomatoes in oil**

**bunch of fresh mixed
herbs, finely chopped**

1 tbsp sunflower oil

1 Preheat the oven to 160°C/325°F/Gas Mark 3. Using a ham knife, fish filleting knife or other knife with a strong, thin blade, pierce the centre of the beef from one side. Twist the knife in circles until you have drilled a tunnel about 1 cm/½ inch wide all the way through.

2 Mix the sun-dried tomatoes and herbs together in a bowl. Spoon the mixture into the tunnel, pushing it in with your fingers or the handle of a wooden spoon.

3 Heat the oil in a flameproof casserole dish, add the beef and cook over a high heat, turning frequently, for 5–8 minutes, or until evenly browned on all sides. Transfer the casserole dish to the oven and roast, basting occasionally, for 20–25 minutes for rare beef, 30–35 minutes for medium rare and 45–55 minutes for well done.

4 Remove the beef from the oven and leave to cool completely before slicing and serving.

Beef Braised in Beer

INGREDIENTS

main

4 tbsp sunflower oil

3 onions, sliced into rings

1 kg/2 lb 4 oz braising steak, cut into 4 pieces

300 ml/10 fl oz Guinness or other stout

storecupboard

salt and pepper

serves ④

1 Preheat the oven to 150°C/300°F/Gas Mark 2. Heat half the oil in a frying pan, add the onions and cook over a low heat, stirring occasionally, for 10 minutes or until softened and light golden brown. Remove the onions with a slotted spoon and reserve.

2 Add the remaining oil to the pan and increase the heat to medium. Add the braising steak, in batches if necessary, and cook, turning occasionally, for 8–10 minutes until browned all over.

3 Put half the onions in the base of a casserole dish. Add the braising steak, season with salt and pepper and top with the remaining onions. Pour in the Guinness, cover and cook in the oven for 3 hours, or until the meat is very tender. Serve straight from the casserole dish.

Pork & Potatoes in Red Wine

INGREDIENTS

main

4 pork chops

**700 g/1 lb 9 oz waxy
potatoes, cut into
large pieces**

**1 tsp coriander seeds,
crushed**

400 ml/14 fl oz red wine

storecupboard

salt and pepper

serves ❹

1 Trim the fat from the chops and melt it in a
non-stick frying pan. Add the potatoes and
cook over a medium-low heat, stirring and
turning occasionally, for 20 minutes until
golden brown all over. Remove from the pan
with a slotted spoon and place in a flameproof
casserole dish.

2 Add the chops to the pan and cook over a
medium heat, turning occasionally, for 8–10
minutes until evenly browned all over. Transfer
to the casserole dish.

3 Gently stir the coriander seeds into the
casserole dish, season with salt and pepper
and pour in the red wine. Bring to the boil,
then reduce the heat, cover and simmer for
40 minutes, or until the meat is tender. Serve
immediately, straight from the casserole dish.

Lamb with Roquefort & Walnut Butter

INGREDIENTS

main

55 g/2 oz unsalted butter

140 g/5 oz Roquefort cheese, crumbled

2 tbsp finely chopped walnuts

8 lamb noisettes

storecupboard

salt and pepper

snipped chives, to garnish (optional)

serves ❹

1 Cream half the butter in a bowl with a wooden spoon. Beat in the cheese and walnuts until thoroughly combined and season to taste with salt and pepper. Turn out the flavoured butter onto a sheet of greaseproof paper and shape into a cylinder. Wrap and leave to chill in the refrigerator until firm.

2 Heat a ridged griddle pan, add the remaining butter and as soon as it has melted, add the lamb noisettes. Then cook for 4–5 minutes on each side.

3 Transfer the lamb to warmed serving plates and top each noisette with a slice of Roquefort and walnut butter. Serve immediately with snipped chives, to garnish, if using.

Irish Stew

INGREDIENTS

serves **4** to **6**

main

1.3 kg/3 lb potatoes, peeled

1 kg/2 lb 4 oz best end of neck or other stewing lamb, trimmed of fat

500 g/1 lb 2 oz onions, thinly sliced

2 tbsp chopped fresh parsley

storecupboard

850 ml/1½ pints water

salt and pepper

1 Thinly slice half the potatoes. Make alternating layers of lamb, onions and sliced potatoes in a large saucepan, seasoning each layer with salt and pepper. Pour in the water so that the layers are just covered.

2 Bring to the boil, then reduce the heat, cover and simmer gently for 1¾ hours. Cut the remaining potatoes into quarters and place on top of the stew to steam. Re-cover the pan and simmer for a further 45 minutes, or until the potato quarters are tender.

3 Arrange the steamed potatoes around the outside of a warmed serving dish. Place the meat, onions and sliced potatoes in the centre. Taste the cooking liquid and adjust the seasoning, if necessary, then spoon it over the meat. Sprinkle with the parsley and serve immediately.

Greek Lamb Patties

INGREDIENTS

main

1 kg/2 lb 4 oz minced lamb

1 onion, grated

½ tsp freshly grated nutmeg

**140 g/5 oz pine kernels,
roughly chopped**

storecupboard

salt and pepper

serves ❹ to ❻

1 Preheat the grill. Put all the ingredients in a bowl and season with salt and pepper. Mix thoroughly with your hands until combined, then shape into 12 patties.

2 Place the patties on a grill rack and cook under the grill for 8 minutes on each side until golden brown and cooked through. Serve immediately.

Bacon-wrapped Sausages

INGREDIENTS

serves **4**

main

8 pork sausages

2 tbsp mild mustard

24 ready-to-eat prunes

8 rashers smoked bacon

1 Preheat the grill. Using a sharp knife, cut a slit along the length of each sausage about three-quarters of the way through. Spread the mustard inside the slits and press 3 prunes into each sausage.

2 Stretch the bacon with the back of a knife until each rasher is quite thin. Wrap a rasher of bacon around each sausage.

3 Place the sausages on a grill rack and cook under the grill, turning occasionally, for 15–20 minutes until cooked through and browned all over. Serve immediately.

Tagliatelle with Ham

INGREDIENTS

main

450 g/1 lb fresh or dried tagliatelle

175 g/6 oz unsalted butter

350 g/12 oz prosciutto, cut into 5-cm/2-inch strips

175 g/6 oz Parmesan cheese, grated

storecupboard

salt and pepper

serves ❹

1 If you are using dried tagliatelle, cook it in a large saucepan of boiling salted water for 10–12 minutes, or until tender but still firm to the bite. If you are using fresh tagliatelle, it will be ready in 2–3 minutes after the water has come back to the boil.

2 Meanwhile, melt the butter in a frying pan. Add the prosciutto and cook over a medium heat, stirring constantly, for 5 minutes. Remove the pan from the heat.

3 Drain the tagliatelle and tip it into a warmed serving dish. Add the prosciutto and melted butter and toss well. Sprinkle evenly with the grated Parmesan cheese, season with pepper and serve.

Chicken Roll

INGREDIENTS

serves ❹

main

115 g/4 oz minced veal

4 skinless, boneless chicken breast portions, about 125 g/4½ oz each

225 g/8 oz Boursin or other cream cheese flavoured with garlic and herbs

3 tbsp clear honey

storecupboard

salt and pepper

sage leaves, to garnish (optional)

1 Put the minced veal in a saucepan and cook over a medium-low heat, stirring frequently, for 5 minutes until evenly browned and broken up. Season with salt and pepper and remove the pan from the heat. Leave to cool.

2 Preheat the oven to 190°C/375°F/Gas Mark 5. Spread out a sheet of clingfilm and place the chicken portions on top, side by side. Cover with another sheet of clingfilm and beat gently with a meat mallet until the portions form a continuous sheet about 1 cm/½ inch thick.

3 Remove the chicken from the clingfilm and spread the cheese over one side of it. Spoon the minced veal evenly over the top. Roll up the chicken from one short side and brush with the honey. Serve immediately garnised with sage leaves, if using.

4 Place the chicken roll in a roasting tin and cook for 1 hour, or until tender and cooked through. Transfer the chicken roll to a chopping board and cut into thin slices. Serve immediately, garnished with sage leaves, if using.

Pan-fried Chicken with Golden Sauce

INGREDIENTS

serves **4**

main

2 mangoes

400 g/14 oz canned apricots in juice

55 g/2 oz unsalted butter

4 skinless, boneless chicken breasts, about 175 g/6 oz each

storecupboard

salt and pepper

1 Using a sharp knife, slice off the sides of the mangoes as close to the stones as possible. Cut through the flesh in the half shells in a criss-cross pattern, turn inside out and cut off the flesh. Cut off any remaining flesh from the stones. Place in a food processor.

2 Drain the apricots, reserving 250 ml/9 fl oz of the can juice. Put the apricots and reserved juice into the food processor and process until smooth. Pour the sauce into a small saucepan.

3 Melt the butter in a large, heavy-based frying pan. Add the chicken and cook over a medium-low heat, turning occasionally, for 15 minutes until golden all over and cooked through. Test by piercing the thickest part with the point of a sharp knife. If the juices run clear, the chicken is cooked.

4 Meanwhile, place the saucepan of sauce over a low heat to warm through, but not boil.

5 Slice the chicken portions diagonally and arrange on warmed serving plates. Spoon the sauce over them and serve immediately, seasoned with pepper.

Chicken & Apricots

INGREDIENTS

serves ❹

main

40 g/1½ oz plain flour

4 chicken portions

4 tbsp olive oil

350 g/12 oz dried apricots, soaked overnight in 600 ml/1 pint water

storecupboard

salt and pepper

1 Spread out the flour on a plate and season with salt and pepper. Roll the chicken portions in the flour to coat, shaking off any excess. Reserve the remaining seasoned flour.

2 Heat the oil in a flameproof casserole dish, add the chicken and cook over a medium heat, turning occasionally, for 8–10 minutes until golden brown. Remove with a slotted spoon and set aside.

3 Drain the apricots, reserving the soaking liquid. Add the reserved flour to the casserole dish and cook over a low heat, stirring constantly, for 2 minutes. Gradually stir in the reserved soaking liquid and bring to the boil, whilst stirring constantly.

4 Add the apricots and return the chicken to the casserole dish. Cover and simmer gently for 45 minutes, or until the chicken is tender and cooked through. Test by piercing the thickest part with the point of a knife. If the juices run clear, the chicken is ready. Serve immediately.

Chicken in a Salt Crust

INGREDIENTS

serves **4**

main

bunch of fresh flat-leaf parsley

1 chicken, about 1.5 kg/3 lb 5 oz

1.5 kg/3 lb 5 oz sea salt

1 egg white

storecupboard

pepper

lemon wedges

fresh thyme sprigs, to garnish (optional)

1 Preheat the oven to 180°C/350°F/Gas Mark 4. Line a roasting tin, large enough to hold the chicken, with a double thickness of foil, letting it overhang the sides. Put the parsley in the cavity of the chicken and tie the legs with kitchen string.

2 Mix the sea salt and egg white together in a bowl until thoroughly combined and the salt is moist. Spoon a layer of the salt mixture into the prepared tin, spreading it out evenly. Place the chicken on top and cover with the remaining salt mixture to cover it completely.

3 Fold the overhanging sides of foil over the chicken to enclose it completely and bake for 1½ hours.

4 Remove the chicken, still wrapped in foil, from the roasting tin. Open the foil and break the salt crust with the back of a large knife. Brush away all traces of salt and transfer the chicken to a carving board. Serve immediately, garnished with thyme, if using.

Lemon Roast Chicken

INGREDIENTS

main

**1 chicken, about
1.5 kg/3 lb 5 oz**

**1 fresh bouquet garni or
6 fresh tarragon sprigs**

1 lemon

**20 g/¾ oz unsalted
butter, softened**

storecupboard

5 tbsp water

salt and pepper

serves ❹

1 Preheat the oven to 200°C/400°F/Gas Mark 6.
Place a rack in a roasting tin for the chicken.

2 Season the chicken inside and out with
salt and pepper. Put the herbs in the cavity.
Squeeze the juice from one half of the lemon
into the cavity, then add the squeezed half.
Tie the chicken legs with kitchen string.

3 Rub the butter over the chicken and transfer
to the rack. Squeeze over the juice from the
remaining lemon half. Roast for 1½ hours,
or until cooked through and tender. Test by
piercing the thickest part with the point of a
knife. If the juices run clear, the chicken is
cooked.

4 Remove the chicken from the tin, tent with
foil and leave to stand for 15 minutes. Remove
the rack from the roasting tin.

5 Skim off the fat from the cooking juices with
a metal spoon and place the tin over a medium
heat. Pour in the water and bring to the boil,
stirring, and scraping any sediment from the
base of the tin with a wooden spoon. Strain the
gravy into a gravyboat. Carve the chicken into
slices and serve with the gravy.

Thai Chicken

INGREDIENTS

serves **4**

main

6 garlic cloves, roughly chopped

8 chicken legs

1 tbsp Thai fish sauce

4 tbsp dark soy sauce

storecupboard

pepper

matchsticks of fresh ginger, to garnish (optional)

1 Put the garlic cloves in a mortar, add 1 teaspoon of black pepper and pound to a paste with a pestle. Using a sharp knife, make 3–4 diagonal slashes on both sides of the chicken legs. Spread the garlic paste over the chicken legs and place them in a dish. Add the fish sauce and soy sauce and turn the legs to coat well. Cover with clingfilm and leave to marinate in the refrigerator for 2 hours.

2 Preheat the grill. Drain the chicken legs, reserving the marinade. Put them on a grill rack and cook under the grill, turning and basting frequently with the reserved marinade, for 20–25 minutes, or until cooked through and tender. Test by piercing the thickest part with the point of a knife. If the juices run clear, the chicken is cooked. Serve immediately garnished with matchsticks of ginger, if using.

Honeyed Duck with Grapefruit

INGREDIENTS

main

1 grapefruit

4 duck breast fillets

4 tbsp clear honey

fresh thyme sprigs, to garnish

storecupboard

salt and pepper

serves ❹

1 Preheat the grill. Peel the grapefruit, removing all traces of the white pith. Using a small, sharp knife, cut out each segment between the membranes. Reserve.

2 Using a sharp knife, make 3 deep diagonal slashes on the skin side of the duck breasts. Brush the duck all over with honey and season with salt and pepper.

3 Place the duck breasts, skin-side down, in a flameproof dish, and cook under the grill for 2 minutes. Remove the dish from the grill and turn the duck over. Put a grapefruit segment in each of the slashes, pressing it in firmly. Brush with the remaining honey and grill for a further 3 minutes.

4 Serve the duck immediately, garnished with the thyme sprigs.

Devilled Turkey Legs

INGREDIENTS

main

2 turkey legs, skinned

½ tsp cayenne pepper

2 tbsp Dijon or hot mustard

40 g/1½ oz unsalted butter, softened

storecupboard

salt and pepper

serves ❹

1 Make deep criss-cross slashes in the turkey legs. Season with salt and pepper and sprinkle with a little of the cayenne pepper. Spread the mustard all over the legs, pressing it well into the slashes. Place the legs in a large, deep dish, cover with clingfilm and leave to marinate in the refrigerator for 6–8 hours.

2 Meanwhile, cream the butter in a bowl, then beat in the remaining cayenne pepper to taste. Cover the bowl with clingfilm and leave until you are ready to serve.

3 Preheat the grill. Place the turkey legs on a grill rack and cook under the grill, turning frequently, for 15–20 minutes, or until golden brown and cooked through. Test by inserting the point of a sharp knife in the thickest part. If the juices run clear, the turkey is cooked.

4 Transfer the turkey legs to a carving board and carve into slices. Arrange on a serving plate with the cayenne butter. Then serve immediately.

4 Vegetables & Vegetarian Dishes

The recipes in this chapter include inspiring accompaniments, flavoursome vegetarian main courses and a tempting selection of salads. As well as an extensive range of vegetables, the recipes also feature eggs, cheese, pasta and rice and many can be served on their own or mixed and matched with some of the dishes from earlier chapters.

Hot Roast Peppers

INGREDIENTS

serves **6**

main

6 red peppers, deseeded and cut into thick strips

140 g/5 oz fresh green serrano or jalapeño chillies, deseeded and sliced into thin strips

2 garlic cloves, crushed

4 tbsp extra virgin olive oil

1 Preheat the oven to 200°C/400°F/Gas Mark 6. Make alternating layers of peppers, chillies and garlic in a shallow casserole dish. Pour in the olive oil.

2 Cover and bake for 50–60 minutes, or until the peppers have softened. Remove the lid and reduce the temperature to 180°C/350°F/Gas Mark 4. Return the casserole dish to the oven and bake for a further 45 minutes, or until the peppers are very soft and beginning to char.

3 Serve immediately if serving hot. Alternatively, leave to cool, then transfer to a large screw-top jar and store in the refrigerator for up to 3 weeks, topped up with more olive oil to keep the peppers covered, if necessary.

Baked Mushrooms

INGREDIENTS

main

40 g/1½ oz unsalted butter

600 ml/1 pint double cream

350 g/12 oz mixed mushrooms, trimmed and halved if large

55 g/2 oz pecorino cheese, grated

storecupboard

salt and pepper

serves 4

1 Preheat the oven to 200°C/400°F/Gas Mark 6. Spread the butter over the base and sides of 4 individual gratin dishes.

2 Spoon a little of the cream into each dish and divide the mushrooms among them. Season to taste with salt and pepper. Spoon the remaining cream over the top and sprinkle with the pecorino cheese.

3 Bake for 15 minutes, or until the cheese is golden brown and bubbling. Serve immediately.

Tomato & Aubergine Layers

INGREDIENTS

serves 4

main

3 tbsp olive oil

2 aubergines, thinly sliced

4 tomatoes, peeled and sliced

3 tbsp chopped fresh flat-leaf parsley

storecupboard

salt and pepper

1 Preheat the oven to 190°C/375°F/Gas Mark 5. Heat the oil in a large frying pan, add the aubergine slices, in batches if necessary, and cook over a medium-low heat, turning once or twice, for 4 minutes. Remove with a fish slice or spatula.

2 Make alternating layers of tomato slices, parsley and aubergine slices in a casserole dish, seasoning each layer with salt and pepper and ending with a layer of tomatoes.

3 Cover and bake for 1 hour or until the vegetables are tender. Serve immediately.

Eggs in Potato Shells

INGREDIENTS

main

4 large baking potatoes

55 g/2 oz butter

2 tbsp single cream

4 eggs

storecupboard

salt and pepper

serves ❹

1 Preheat the oven to 200°C/400°F/Gas Mark 6. Prick the potatoes with a fork and bake for 1 hour, or until soft.

2 Remove the potatoes from the oven but do not switch the oven off. Cut each potato, lengthways, in half and carefully use a teaspoon to scoop out the flesh into a bowl, without piercing the shells. Mash the flesh with the butter and cream and season with salt and pepper.

3 Pile the mashed potato back into the shells and place them in an ovenproof dish that will hold them steady. Make a hollow in the centre of each and break in an egg. Season with salt and pepper.

4 Put the dish in the oven and bake for 10–15 minutes, or until the eggs are just set. Then serve immediately.

Soufflé Cauliflower Cheese

INGREDIENTS

main

650 g/1 lb 7 oz cauliflower, cut into florets

4 eggs, separated

115 g/4 oz blue cheese, crumbled

2 tsp Dijon mustard

storecupboard

salt and pepper

serves ❹

1 Preheat the oven to 190°C/375°F/Gas Mark 5. Cook the cauliflower in a large saucepan of salted boiling water for 5–10 minutes, or until just tender. Drain well, refresh under cold running water and drain again.

2 Put the cauliflower florets and egg yolks into a food processor and process until smooth and combined. Transfer the mixture to a bowl and stir in the cheese and mustard. Season with salt and pepper.

3 Whisk the egg whites in a grease-free bowl until stiff. Using a rubber spatula, gently fold about one-third of the egg whites into the cauliflower mixture. Fold in the remaining egg whites in 2 batches.

4 Transfer the mixture to individual soufflé dishes and bake for 35 minutes, or until well risen and golden brown on top. Serve immediately.

Mixed Potato Rösti

INGREDIENTS

main

325 g/11½ oz potatoes

325 g/11½ oz sweet potatoes

4 tbsp sunflower oil

40 g/1½ oz butter

storecupboard

salt

serves ❹

1 Parboil the ordinary potatoes in a large saucepan of salted water for 10 minutes, then drain and leave to cool. Meanwhile, peel and coarsely grate the sweet potatoes into a bowl. When the parboiled potatoes have cooled, peel and coarsely grate into another bowl.

2 Divide the potatoes and the sweet potatoes separately into 4 equal portions and shape each portion into a pattie about 1 cm/½ inch thick, pressing them together firmly.

3 Heat half the oil with half the butter in a heavy-based frying pan. Add the potato rösti and cook over a medium heat for 5 minutes, or until crisp and golden on the undersides. Turn them carefully with a fish slice or spatula, pat into shape if necessary, and cook for a further 5 minutes, or until golden brown on the second side. Remove from the pan and keep warm.

4 Heat the remaining oil and butter in the pan. Add the sweet potato rösti and cook for 5 minutes on each side as before. Remove from the pan and serve both types of potato rösti immediately.

Pasta with Tomatoes & Spinach

INGREDIENTS

main

450 g/1 lb dried orecchiette or other pasta shapes

3 tbsp olive oil

225 g/8 oz fresh baby spinach leaves, tough stalks removed

450 g/1 lb cherry tomatoes, halved

storecupboard

salt and pepper

Parmesan cheese, grated (optional)

serves ❹

1 Cook the pasta in a large saucepan of boiling salted water for 10–12 minutes, or until tender but still firm to the bite.

2 Heat the oil in a saucepan, add the spinach and tomatoes and cook, gently stirring occasionally, for 2–3 minutes, or until the spinach has wilted and the tomatoes are heated through but not disintegrating.

3 Drain the pasta and add it to the pan of vegetables. Toss gently, season with salt and pepper, sprinkle over some Parmesan cheese, if using, and serve immediately.

Spaghetti with Parsley & Parmesan

INGREDIENTS

main

450 g/1 lb dried spaghetti

175 g/6 oz unsalted butter

4 tbsp chopped fresh flat-leaf parsley

225 g/8 oz Parmesan cheese, grated

storecupboard

salt

serves ❹

1 Cook the pasta in a large saucepan of boiling salted water for 10–12 minutes, or until tender but still firm to the bite. Drain and tip into a warmed serving dish.

2 Add the butter, parsley and half the Parmesan cheese and toss well, using 2 forks, until the butter and cheese have melted. Serve immediately with the remaining Parmesan cheese handed separately.

Leeks with Cheese & Eggs

INGREDIENTS

serves ❹

main

85 g/3 oz unsalted butter

8 leeks, trimmed

6 tbsp freshly grated Parmesan cheese

4 eggs

storecupboard

salt and pepper

1 Preheat the oven to 160°C/325°F/Gas Mark 3. Grease an ovenproof dish with a little of the butter.

2 Bring a large saucepan of salted water to the boil, add the leeks and cook for 7–10 minutes, or until tender but still firm to the bite. Drain well and carefully squeeze out as much water as possible. Pat dry with kitchen paper.

3 Place the leeks in the prepared dish. Sprinkle with half the Parmesan cheese and dot with one-third of the remaining butter. Bake in the oven for 5 minutes.

4 Meanwhile, melt the remaining butter in a frying pan. Add the eggs, one at a time, and cook until the whites are just set. Remove the leeks from the oven and, using a fish slice or spatula, top with the eggs. Pour the butter from the pan over them, sprinkle with the remaining Parmesan cheese and season with pepper. Serve immediately.

Cheese & Vegetable Tart

INGREDIENTS

serves 4

main

350 g/12 oz ready-made shortcrust pastry, thawed if frozen

280 g/10 oz mixed frozen vegetables

150 ml/5 fl oz double cream

115 g/4 oz Cheddar cheese, grated

storecupboard

salt and pepper

1 Thinly roll out the dough on a lightly floured work surface and use to line a 23-cm/9-inch quiche tin. Prick the base and chill in the refrigerator for 30 minutes. Preheat the oven to 200°C/400°F/Gas Mark 6.

2 Line the pastry case with foil and half-fill with baking beans. Place the tin on a baking sheet and bake for 15–20 minutes, or until just firm. Remove the beans and foil, return the pastry case to the oven and bake for a further 5–7 minutes until golden. Remove the pastry case from the oven and leave to cool in the tin.

3 Meanwhile, cook the frozen vegetables in a saucepan of salted boiling water. Drain and leave to cool.

4 When ready to cook, preheat the oven again to 200°C/400°F/Gas Mark 6. Mix the cooked vegetables and cream together and season with salt and pepper. Spoon the mixture evenly into the pastry case and sprinkle with the cheese. Bake for 15 minutes, or until the cheese has melted and is turning golden. Serve hot or cold.

Mexican Rice

INGREDIENTS

serves ❹

main

1 onion, chopped

400 g/14 oz plum tomatoes, peeled, deseeded and chopped

250 ml/9 fl oz beef stock

200 g/7 oz long-grain rice

storecupboard

salt and pepper

1 Put the onion and tomatoes in a food processor and process to a smooth purée. Scrape the purée into a saucepan, pour in the stock and bring to the boil over a medium heat, stirring occasionally.

2 Add the rice and stir once, then reduce the heat, cover and simmer for 20–25 minutes until all the liquid has been absorbed and the rice is tender. Season to taste with salt and pepper and serve immediately.

Tomatoes with Goat's Cheese

INGREDIENTS

main

12 tomatoes

6 round goat's cheeses, such as Rocamadour, about 40 g/ 1½ oz each

3 fresh basil sprigs, chopped

1 egg, lightly beaten

storecupboard

salt and pepper

serves 6

1 Slice the tops off the tomatoes at the stalk end and reserve. Scoop out the flesh and seeds with a teaspoon, taking care not to pierce the tomato shells. Discard the tomato seeds and put the flesh in a bowl. Sprinkle the inside of each tomato shell with a pinch of salt, turn upside down on kitchen paper and leave to drain for 45 minutes.

2 Add the cheese and basil to the tomato flesh in the bowl and mash well until thoroughly combined. Season with salt and pepper and beat in the egg until the mixture is thick and sticky.

3 Preheat the oven to 160°C/325°F/Gas Mark 3. Spoon the cheese mixture into the tomato shells and replace the lids. Put the tomatoes in an ovenproof dish that will hold them securely and bake for 10 minutes. Turn off the oven but do not remove the tomatoes for 5 minutes, then serve.

Moroccan Tomato & Red Pepper Salad

INGREDIENTS

main

3 red peppers

4 ripe tomatoes

½ bunch of fresh coriander, chopped

2 garlic cloves, finely chopped

storecupboard

salt and pepper

serves ❹

1 Preheat the grill. Place the peppers on a baking sheet and cook under the grill, turning occasionally, for 15 minutes. Add the tomatoes and grill, turning occasionally, for a further 5–10 minutes, or until all the skins are charred and blistered. Remove from the heat and leave to cool.

2 Peel and deseed the peppers and tomatoes and slice the flesh thinly. Place in a bowl, mix well and season with salt and pepper. Sprinkle with the coriander and garlic, cover with clingfilm and chill in the refrigerator for at least 1 hour. Just before serving, drain off any excess liquid.

Onion & Orange Salad

INGREDIENTS

serves **4**

main

4 oranges

2 white onions, thinly sliced and pushed out into rings

16 black olives, stoned

extra virgin olive oil, for drizzling

storecupboard

salt and pepper

1 Peel the oranges, removing all traces of bitter white pith. Using a sharp knife, cut the flesh crossways into slices and remove the pips, if necessary.

2 Arrange the orange slices and onion rings in concentric circles on individual serving plates and season with salt and pepper. Place 4 olives in the centre of each plate and drizzle the salads with olive oil. Cover and leave to stand for 30 minutes before serving.

Tomato & Feta Salad

INGREDIENTS

serves ❹

main

1 kg/2 lb 4 oz ripe tomatoes, thickly sliced

225 g/8 oz feta cheese

125 ml/4 fl oz extra virgin olive oil

16 black olives, stoned

storecupboard

pepper

1 Arrange the tomato slices in concentric rings on a serving dish. Crumble the feta over the tomatoes and drizzle with the olive oil. Top with the olives.

2 Season to taste with pepper. Salt is probably not necessary because feta is already quite salty. Leave to stand for 30 minutes before serving.

Mushroom Salad

INGREDIENTS

main

225 g/8 oz white or pink chestnut mushrooms, thinly sliced

finely grated rind and juice of ½ lemon

3 tbsp crème fraîche

1 tbsp chopped fresh chervil

storecupboard

salt and pepper

serves ❹

1 Put the mushrooms in a large bowl, sprinkle with the lemon rind and juice and toss well. Gently stir in the crème fraîche and season with salt and pepper.

2 Cover the bowl with clingfilm and leave to stand, stirring once or twice, for 1 hour. Spoon the salad into a serving bowl, sprinkle with the chervil and serve.

5 Desserts

For many people a meal is not complete without a sweet treat at the end, although this sometimes seems a course too far for the busy cook. Now, using just four ingredients, you can whip up irresistible cold creamy desserts, mouthwatering hot puddings and even fabulous home-made ices with little effort and superb results.

Layered Nectarine Cream

INGREDIENTS

serves ❹

main

4 nectarines, peeled, stoned and sliced

2 tbsp amaretto liqueur

175 g/6 oz curd cheese

300 ml/10 fl oz peach-flavoured yogurt

1 Reserve a few nectarine slices for decoration. Put the remainder in a bowl, add the liqueur and toss gently, then set aside.

2 Beat the cheese and yogurt together in another bowl until thoroughly combined. Spoon half the mixture into 4 tall glasses. Divide the nectarine and liqueur mixture among them and top with the remaining cheese and yogurt mixture.

3 Decorate with the reserved nectarine slices and leave to chill in the refrigerator for at least 30 minutes before serving.

Summer Pudding

INGREDIENTS

main

900 g/2 lb mixed berries, such as raspberries and blackberries

140 g/5 oz caster sugar

125 ml/4 fl oz milk

8 slices day-old white bread, crusts removed

serves 6

1 Hull the berries and put them in a bowl. Sprinkle with the sugar and set aside.

2 Sprinkle the milk over the slices of bread to soften them slightly. Line the base and sides of a pudding basin with two-thirds of the bread, cutting it to fit but overlap the edges slightly. Spoon the berries into the basin and place the remaining bread slices on top, cutting to fit and making sure that the fruit is completely covered.

3 Place a round of greaseproof paper on top of the last layer of bread. Put a plate or saucer, slightly smaller than the diameter of the basin, on top, then place a weight, such as a heavy can of fruit, on the plate. Leave to chill in the refrigerator for at least 8 hours.

4 To serve, remove the weight, plate and greaseproof paper. Invert a serving dish on top of the basin and, holding them together, reverse and shake sharply and the pudding should slide out.

Honey & Chocolate Bananas

INGREDIENTS

serves **4**

main

55 g/2 oz unsalted butter

4 ripe bananas, peeled and halved lengthways

4 tbsp clear honey

175 g/6 oz plain dark chocolate, grated

1 Melt the butter in a frying pan, add the bananas and cook over a medium-low heat, turning occasionally, for 4–5 minutes. Carefully transfer them to individual serving plates.

2 Drizzle 1 tablespoon of honey along the length of each banana and sprinkle with the grated chocolate. Serve immediately.

Pears in Wine

INGREDIENTS

serves 4

main

4 large pears

225 g/8 oz caster sugar

1 cinnamon stick or vanilla pod

150 ml/5 fl oz red wine

storecupboard

150 ml/5 fl oz water

1 Peel the pears, leaving the stalks intact. Cut a thin slice off the base of each pear so that it will stand upright.

2 Put the sugar and cinnamon stick in a large saucepan, add the water and bring to the boil over a medium heat, stirring until the sugar has dissolved. Add the pears, reduce the heat, cover and then simmer for 15 minutes.

3 Pour in the wine and simmer, uncovered, for a further 15 minutes, or until the pears are just tender. Remove the pears with a slotted spoon and stand them in a serving dish.

4 Remove and discard the cinnamon stick and bring the wine syrup back to the boil. Boil rapidly until thickened, then pour the syrup over the pears and leave to cool. Chill for at least 1 hour before serving.

Raspberries and Meringue Cream

INGREDIENTS

main

500 g/1 lb 2 oz raspberries

4 tbsp amaretto or crème de framboise liqueur

300 ml/10 fl oz double cream

6 small white meringues, coarsely crushed

serves ❹

1 Hull the raspberries, put them in a bowl and sprinkle the liqueur over them. Cover with clingfilm and leave to chill in the refrigerator for 2 hours.

2 Whip the cream in a large bowl until soft peaks form, then fold the raspberries, with their juices, into it. Sprinkle the crushed meringues on top and gently fold in. Spoon into a serving dish and serve immediately.

Citrus Granita

INGREDIENTS

serves ❻

main

6 oranges

1½ lemons

140 g/5 oz sugar

6 amaretti biscuits

storecupboard

450 ml/16 fl oz water

1 Pare the rind from the fruit, cut off and discard the pith, then slice a few thin strips of rind and reserve them separately from the large pieces. Squeeze the juice from the fruit.

2 Boil the sugar and water in a heavy-based saucepan and stir until the sugar dissolves. Boil, without stirring, for 10 minutes until syrupy. Remove from the heat, stir in the large rind pieces, cover and leave to cool.

3 Strain the cooled syrup into a freezerproof container and stir in the juice. Freeze, uncovered, for 4 hours until slushy.

4 Blanch the thin rind strips in a saucepan of boiling water for 2 minutes. Drain and refresh with cold water. Pat dry with kitchen paper.

5 Remove the granita from the freezer and break up with a fork. Freeze again for a further 4 hours, or until hard.

6 Remove the granita from the freezer and leave until slightly softened. Beat with a fork, then spoon into glasses and decorate with the rind strips. Serve with the biscuits.

Blackcurrant Sorbet

INGREDIENTS

main

100 g/3½ oz caster sugar

500 g/1 lb 2 oz blackcurrants

2 tbsp lemon juice

1 tbsp egg white

storecupboard

125 ml/4 fl oz water

serves ❻

1 Boil the water and sugar in a saucepan, stirring until the sugar dissolves. Boil, without stirring, for a further 2 minutes, then remove from the heat and leave to cool.

2 Put the blackcurrants and lemon juice in a food processor and process to a purée. Add the cooled syrup and process to combine. Using a spatula, press the purée through a nylon sieve over a bowl to remove the seeds.

3 Pour the purée into a freezerproof container, cover with clingfilm and freeze for 3–4 hours, or until slushy. Remove from the freezer, chop up and process until the sorbet is smooth. Add the egg white and process until combined.

4 Return the sorbet to the container, re-cover and re-freeze for a further 4 hours, or until almost firm. Remove from the freezer, chop up and process until the sorbet is smooth.

5 Return the sorbet to the container, cover tightly and return to the freezer, where it will keep for up to 5 days. Remove the sorbet from the freezer and leave to stand at room temperature to soften slightly before serving.

Sweet & Sour Fruit Compote

INGREDIENTS

serves ❹

main

650 g/1 lb 7 oz rhubarb, cut into 2.5-cm/1-inch pieces

juice of 2 oranges

70 g/2½ oz vanilla sugar or caster sugar, plus extra to serve

280 g/10 oz strawberries

1 Put the rhubarb in a saucepan, add the orange juice and sugar and bring to the boil, stirring gently, until the sugar has dissolved. Reduce the heat and simmer, stirring occasionally, for 5 minutes.

2 Meanwhile, hull the strawberries and halve any large ones. Add them to the pan and simmer for a further 5 minutes.

3 Divide the warm compote among individual serving bowls and serve immediately or leave to cool to room temperature. Sprinkle with extra sugar before serving.

Lime Snow

INGREDIENTS

main

3 limes

55 g/2 oz caster sugar

1 tbsp powdered gelatine

2 egg whites

storecupboard

250 ml/9 fl oz water

serves ❹

1 Finely grate the rind of one lime. Set aside about one-quarter for decoration and put the remainder in a bowl. Squeeze the juice from all the limes and add to the bowl.

2 Put the sugar in a saucepan, pour in the water and bring to the boil, stirring until the sugar has dissolved. Remove from the heat and sprinkle the gelatine over the liquid. Leave for 5 minutes, then swirl until the gelatine has dissolved completely. Pour the mixture into the bowl of lime juice, in a thin continuous stream, stirring constantly. Refrigerate for 30 minutes until beginning to set.

3 Whisk the egg whites in a grease-free bowl until stiff. Remove the lime jelly from the refrigerator and beat until it is foamy. Gently fold in the egg whites with a spatula in 2 batches. Return the mixture to the refrigerator and chill for a further 15 minutes.

4 Remove the lime snow from the refrigerator and beat until light and fluffy. Divide among dishes and refrigerate for 2–3 hours. Sprinkle with the remaining rind before serving.

Chestnut Cream with Madeira

INGREDIENTS

serves 6

main

6 trifle sponge cakes

175 ml/6 fl oz Madeira

350 g/12 oz canned sweetened chestnut purée

225 ml/8 fl oz double cream

1 Place a trifle sponge in each of 6 glasses, trimming it to fit if necessary. Spoon the Madeira over the sponges and leave to stand for 15 minutes.

2 Divide the chestnut purée among the glasses and smooth the surface with the back of a spoon. If necessary, wipe the rims of the glasses with damp kitchen paper.

3 Whip the cream in a bowl until stiff, then spoon into a piping bag fitted with a star-shaped nozzle. Pipe the cream decoratively over the chestnut purée. Then leave to chill in the refrigerator for at least 30 minutes before serving.

Apricot Swirl

INGREDIENTS

main

400 g/14 oz canned apricots in fruit juice, drained

1 tbsp amaretto or Cointreau liqueur

175 ml/6 fl oz thick crème fraîche

2 tbsp chopped pistachio nuts

serves ❹

1 Put the apricots and liqueur in a food processor and process to a purée. Put alternate spoonfuls of purée and crème fraîche into 4 glasses, swirling them together gently to create marbling.

2 Sprinkle the pistachio nuts over the top to decorate and serve immediately. Alternatively, leave to chill in the refrigerator for 30–45 minutes before serving.

Index

Apple
  Baked Apples with Ginger
    170
Apricot
  Apricot Swirl 168
  Chicken & Apricots 100
Artichokes with Parsley Butter
  36
Asparagus
  Easy Asparagus Soup 14
  Ham & Asparagus Rolls 26
Aubergine
  Aubergine Pâté 34
  Tomato & Aubergine Layers
    118
Avocado Soup 20

Bacon
  Bacon Rolls 24
  Bacon-wrapped Sausages
    92
Banana
  Honey & Chocolate Bananas
    152
Beef
  Beef Braised in Beer 82
  Beef Consommé with Eggs
    and Parmesan 10
  Peppered Steak 78
  Stuffed Beef Fillet 80
Berries
  Blackcurrant Sorbet 160
  Raspberries and Meringue
    Cream 156
  Summer Pudding 150
  Sweet & Sour Fruit
    Compote 162

Cauliflower
  Soufflé Cauliflower Cheese
    122
Cheese
  Cheese & Vegetable Tart
    132
  Griddled Salmon with
    Cheese 46
  Lamb with Roquefort &
    Walnut Butter 86
  Leeks with Cheese & Eggs
    130

Soufflé Cauliflower Cheese
  122
Spinach & Cheese Soup 12
Tomato & Feta Salad 142
Tomatoes with Goat's
  Cheese 136
Chestnut Cream with Madeira
  166
Chicken
  Chicken & Apricots 100
  Chicken Roll 96
  Chicken in a Salt Crust 102
  Lemon Roast Chicken 104
  Pan-fried Chicken with
    Golden Sauce 98
  Thai Chicken 106
Chorizo with Parsley & Olives
  28
Citrus fruit
  Red Pepper & Orange Soup
    22
  Citrus Granita 158
  Honeyed Duck with
    Grapefruit 108
  Lemon Roast Chicken 104
  Lime Snow 164
  Onion & Orange Salad 140
  Prawns in Orange Juice 72

Duck
  Honeyed Duck with
    Grapefruit 108

Eggs
  Beef Consommé with Eggs
    and Parmesan 10
  Eggs in Potato Shells 120
  Leeks with Cheese & Eggs
    130

Fish
  Baked Fish with Preserved
    Lemons 60
  Baked Snapper 42
  Griddled Salmon with
    Cheese 46
  Marinated Monkfish Kebabs
    52
  Oven-baked Swordfish
    Steaks 44
  Plaice in Cream Sauce 40
  Salmon & Herbs in
    Prosciutto Parcels 48

Sea Bream with Tomatoes,
  Yogurt & Spinach 62
Skate with Caper Berries
  56
Sole with Mushrooms 50
Swordfish with a Crisp
  Tomato Topping 54
Teriyaki Tuna 58

Ham
  Ham & Asparagus Rolls 26
  Salmon & Herbs in
    Prosciutto Parcels 48
  Tagliatelle with Ham 94

Lamb
  Greek Lamb Patties 90
  Irish Stew 88
  Lamb with Roquefort &
    Walnut Butter 86
Leek
  Leek & Potato Soup 18
  Leeks with Cheese & Eggs
    130

Melon & Morello Cherries
  172
Mushroom
  Baked Mushrooms 116
  Mushroom Salad 144
  Sole with Mushrooms 50

Nachos with Chillies & Olives
  32
Nectarine
  Layered Nectarine Cream
    148

Onion & Orange Salad 140

Pasta
  Pasta with Tomatoes &
    Spinach 126
  Spaghetti with Parsley &
    Parmesan 128
  Tagliatelle with Ham 94
Pea
  Cream of Pea Soup 16
Pear
  Pears in Wine 154
Peppers
  Red Pepper & Orange Soup
    22
  Hot Roast Peppers 114

Moroccan Tomato & Red
  Pepper Salad 138
Pineapple
  Mexican Pineapple Custard
    174
Pork & Potatoes in Red Wine
  84
Potato
  Eggs in Potato Shells 120
  Leek & Potato Soup 18
  Mixed Potato Rösti 124
  Pork & Potatoes in Red
    Wine 84

Rhubarb
  Sweet & Sour Fruit
    Compote 162
Rice
  Mexican Rice 134

Seafood
  Hot Chilli Prawns 74
  Mussels with Garlic &
    Parsley Butter 66
  Mustard Prawns 70
  Normandy Cream Mussels
    64
  Prawns in Orange Juice 72
  Scallops in Vermouth 68
Spinach
  Pasta with Tomatoes &
    Spinach 126
  Sea Bream with Tomatoes,
    Yogurt & Spinach 62
  Spinach & Cheese Soup 12

Tomato
  Moroccan Tomato & Red
    Pepper Salad 138
  Pasta with Tomatoes &
    Spinach 126
  Sea Bream with Tomatoes,
    Yogurt & Spinach 62
  Swordfish with a Crisp
    Tomato Topping 54
  Tomato & Aubergine Layers
    118
  Tomato & Feta Salad 142
  Tomato Bruschetta 30
  Tomatoes with Goat's
    Cheese 136
Turkey
  Devilled Turkey Legs 110

Mexican Pineapple Custard

INGREDIENTS

main

450 g/1 lb canned pineapple in juice, drained

600 ml/1 pint milk

6 eggs

115 g/4 oz caster sugar

serves 6

1 Preheat the oven to 160°C/325°F/Gas Mark 3. Roughly chop the pineapple, place in a food processor, in batches if necessary, and process briefly to a purée.

2 Pour the milk into a saucepan and heat gently to just below boiling point. Remove the pan from the heat.

3 Separate 2 of the eggs and place the yolks in a heatproof bowl. Add the remaining eggs and the sugar. Place the bowl over a saucepan of barely simmering water and whisk until the mixture is thickened and pale. (Make sure the bowl does not touch the water.) Remove the bowl from the pan and add the milk in a thin stream, stirring constantly. Stir in the purée.

4 Pour the mixture into an ovenproof dish and put the dish in a roasting tin. Add boiling water to about halfway up the sides of the dish and bake for 45–50 minutes, or until a cocktail stick inserted into the custard comes out clean.

5 Remove the dish from the roasting tin and serve immediately.

Melon & Morello Cherries

INGREDIENTS

main

2 ogen melons

400–425 g/14–15 oz canned morello cherries, drained

2 tbsp kirsch

450 ml/16 fl oz peach sorbet or flavour of your choice

serves ❹

1 Halve the melons horizontally and scoop out the seeds with a spoon. Using a melon baller, scoop out the flesh, leaving shells about 5 mm/ ¼ inch thick. Set the shells aside, put the melon balls in a bowl and chill in the refrigerator for 1 hour.

2 Meanwhile, mix the cherries and kirsch together in another bowl. Cover with clingfilm and leave to macerate for 1 hour.

3 Add the chilled melon to the cherry mixture. Using the melon baller, scoop the sorbet into balls and add to the fruit mixture. Stir well, divide the mixture among the melon shells and serve immediately.

Baked Apples with Ginger

INGREDIENTS

serves 4

main

40 g/1½ oz unsalted butter, plus extra for greasing

4 large tart apples

4 tbsp plum jam

3 tbsp chopped stem ginger

storecupboard

300 ml/10 fl oz water

1 Preheat the oven to 190°C/375°F/Gas Mark 5. Grease a shallow ovenproof dish, large enough to hold all the apples steady, with butter.

2 Using an apple corer, core the apples without cutting all the way through to the base. Peel the top half of each. Using a sharp knife, enlarge the cavity slightly. Place the apples in the prepared dish.

3 Mix the plum jam and stem ginger together in a bowl and spoon the mixture into the cavities. Melt the butter and brush it over the top halves of the apples. Spoon the remainder over the top of the filling.

4 Pour the water into the dish but not over the apples and bake, basting occasionally with the cooking juices, for 45–60 minutes. Serve.